The Coal Life

The Coal Life

Poems by Adam Vines

The University of Arkansas Press
Fayetteville
2012

ISBN-10: 1-55728-980-8
ISBN-13: 978-1-55728-980-3

16   15   14   13   12   1   2   3   4   5

Text design by Ellen Beeler

⊛ The paper used in this publication meets the minimum requirements
of the American National Standard for Permanence of Paper for
Printed Library Materials Z39.48—84.

Library of Congress Cataloging-in-Publication Data

Vines, Adam.
   The coal life : poems / by Adam Vines.
      p. cm.
   ISBN 978-1-55728-980-3 (pbk. : alk. paper)
   I. Title.
   PS3622.I55C63 2012
   811'.6—dc23
                                                      2011048103

For Daddy, Jeff, and my three Ms

Acknowledgments

I am forever grateful to the following people: William Logan, Debora Greger, Michael Hofmann, Sidney Wade, Jim Mersmann, Bob Collins, Tony Crunk, Enid Shomer, Rebecca Bach, Mark Jeffreys, Danny Anderson, Greg Fraser, Tina Harris, Jim Paxson, Manny Blacksher, Jim Owens, Rob Short, Allen Jih, Jason Slatton, Alan Shapiro, Claudia Emerson, Mary Jo Salter, Wyatt Prunty, my Sewanee family, my UF family, my UAB family, and the Vines, Ferguson, and Paddock families—especially the storytellers: Aunt Frances, Uncle Frank, Aunt Norma, Granddaddy, and Grandmother.

I would like to thank the editors of the following publications in which some of these poems originally appeared. *32 Poems,* "Toilet Flowers"; *The American Poetry Journal,* "La Mar es una Puta"; *Apalachee Review,* "Red Mountains"; *Aura,* "Path," "Ashes and Dust," "Mantrip," "The Other Woman"; *The Chariton Review,* "Worm Grunters," "After Bloody Mary's Death," "The Baptist Steeple," "Tracks"; *The Cincinnati Review,* "The Old Salt's Brag"; *Controlled Burn,* "On Speaking with an Old Classmate after his Physics Lecture at a Local University"; *A Face to Meet the Faces: An Anthology of Contemporary Persona Poetry,* "Hamlet Beside the Stream"; *Family Matters: Poems of Our Families,* "Grabbing"; *Flint Hills Review,* "Some Like It Hot"; *The Greensboro Review,* "Back Door"; *Hunger Mountain,* "Magritte's Daemon"; *Iron Horse Literary Review,* "Mountain of Fire"; *Isotope,* "Coaxing the Coal Back to Life"; *Kennesaw Review,* "Darwin Dreams of the Second Coming"; *The Literary Review,* "Gauguin's Bed"; *Louisiana Literature,* "Reclamation"; *Mêlée,* "Epilogue and Return"; *Meridian,* "Methane"; *Natural Bridge,* "Mine Rats"; *New Delta Review,* "Brick Hammer and Broken Watch,"

"Tulips and Pigs"; *North American Review,* "Eden's Oranges"; *Poet Lore*, "Threat of Spring"; *Post Road*, "Charter," "Floundering"; *Santa Clara Review,* "Putting the Mule Out to Pasture," "Burying the Dead," "Return"; *Sewanee Theological Review*, "Elegy for Jessica Hayden," "The Fox"; *The South Carolina Review*, "Almost Clean"; *South Dakota Review*, "Offerings," "Take Over"; *Southern Indiana Review*, "Stake Horse"; *storySouth,* "Overburden"; *Tampa Review*, "I Wake to Find I Am Not Awake"; *The Texas Review*, "The Motel Room"; *Third Coast,* "Georg Cantor, from Halle Sanatorium, 1884"; *Unsplendid*, "The Cleaving."

Contents

The Coal Life

Prologue and Return

The spotlight from a barge
searching for the bend
fidgets along the riverbank.
A heron's tar-gargling cry
recedes into fog
while an armadillo wobbles
through the thicket
like a lost child.
A snapping turtle snatches
the leg of a mallard—wings slap
the water like oars, trying to pull
free from the unseen snag.
In the pit lined with creek stones,
flames gnaw on split hickory,
hawk out sparks like seeds.
Downhill lie the spine and ribs
of my great-grandfather's ferryboat
I once pretended was the carcass
of an alligator gar,
the swivel chair with straps
that harnessed him
while he rowed—his legs
crushed in a dogtrot mine
when he was a boy. His claim:
we were spawned in the sloughs,
in logjams and stump rows,
under hyacinth and cattail,
and that's where we all return,
to be swallowed slowly
with each year's leaf fall and rot.

3

Red Mountains

I thought, closing my eyes, I would see the mythic boar
rise from the peat, its tufts of willow and hazel scrub,
drumlins jutting from jowls, and Saint Columba dipping wine
from the tenebrous lough below, his Psalter unbolting the doors
to crannogs. But none of these visions was given to me.
Atop Benbulben that December, I saw only the dying

of another year. Sheep plodded down a switchback, rumps
red, yellow, and blue, and as the wind picked up, everything
slipped away except the red ewes hunkered in crannies.

The mountain face turned to clay. From the ridge,
loblolly roots dangled, the longest one stripped to sweet wood,
and my hands, shoes, the knees of my pants ran red.

For a moment, I was suspended above it all. Then it all
returned to peat and sheep, the shadow myth of ruins.
Just today, I recalled the clay bank behind my granddad's shed,

the taproot I used as a rope, and my father's shoulders
as he held me and ran along the ridge after I'd finally climbed
the steepest red mountain in the country, hell, in the world!

Burying the Dead

It always happens like this:
I'm in the backyard burying
my army men and cowboys
in the overburden with a shovel
where the rain uncovered them
since the last ceremony.
I tell myself this time I'll dig deeper.
I wave Mom off like Dad would,
tell her I'm too busy for lunch—
the dead must be buried
because the rain will come again
soon. The storm smears the sky
with gray fists, and I see Dad
circling the church across the street,
tool belt chinking nails, hammer
dangling from a loop in his overalls.
I call to him, but the storm
drowns my voice, the runoff carries
the loose soil away,
the arms of the buried rise again.

Handwritten annotations:

Miners

he sees people going into the mines every day being "buried" but they keep coming back people die in mines

playing grownup

what does he do for work? undertaker?

he is being buried too?

—zombies like the fathers in *Path*

ignores Mom
ignored by Dad

hiding your skeletons/ hiding your past

because of the mining, when people are buried they sometimes resurface

a sense of determination

5

The Baptist Steeple

"Consider that wee shall be as a Citty upon a Hill, the
eies of all people are uppon us."

—*John Winthrop*

I could hear the Italians and Greeks blasting the overburden,
dropping trees for roof chocks from the hill
where I would steal my first kiss and, later that year, pour
blood from my first buck. "We must be a beacon for the lost
       and poor,"
our preacher said. "Idleness is Hell; it's time to unload your
       burdens
into the plate and build a steeple higher than Winthrop's hill."

My mother, who'd traded clacker for bills
at thirty-percent penalty and still got more flour
in town than at the commissary, and my father, who'd worked
       two shifts
a week extra at the tipple, taking off Sunday shifts
to pray for forgiveness and to wash the crucifixion and red flowers
of hope annealed in high windows, forgot their debts and the
       company bills.

The next year, I started picking coal from the spoils
for our stove. After church, the members built scaffolds
and with hammers and nails, their forearms wormed with veins,
climbed closer to God, while Catholic men led blind mules to
       the veins
of coal underground. Our preacher said, "It's their choice, like
       the scaffolds
heretics chose to bear." The steeple never rose above the spoils.

Threat of Spring

When I was eight, the bone blossoms
of the dogwood in our front yard
first marked what should
have been spring, and the flotsam

of spent blooms from Bradford pears
streaking the streets, and the careless
care of buck squirrels chasing
their affections, winding up trunks, lacing

through brake squeals and rubber:
how many times do both meet the same fate?
And I remember that childhood supper—
the one we ate too late—and the rake

of my mother's eyes down every inch of my father
who had the squirrels' fever and would rather
splay himself on the street with a bloody grin
and chalk it up to instinct than admit some moral sin.

Tracks

The day frays
at the hem
where pine tops sway
in the whims

of colors as tenuous
as the sandstone gulley
(a sunset itself) cut and sullied
from last night's rain. The pendulous

hawk must have a home nearby,
its thermals lessening to a sigh.
The beaver heads for its den
on the bank, and the coal barges bend

out of sight. And we too have homes
to tend, meals to prepare, truths
to bend. But for now the loam
holds us steady, and the proof

of our meeting—the impressions
we left behind in our stead—
narrows, funneling us into one: the procession
of the four-legged beast we made.

And if someone were to track our path
to here where we have stopped to rest
(a fallen tree, a crushed bird nest),
the tracker wouldn't find the wrath

of silence replacing words or what we shed
that left no trace. The fork where we divided from feral
one again to two, no trails from where we bled,
might prove the beast upright again, but who's to judge if moral.

Path

[handwritten: work hard hours working for their kids but they don't get to raise them]

*"His kids didn't hardly know him. . . . They were asleep
when he left and they were asleep when he come back."* *[handwritten: she's uneducated]*
—*A miner's wife*

At shift change, children who can't sleep
forget the sky and look to the path for stars. *[handwritten: the lamps]*

[handwritten: what path / look to for the future / coal mine]

On breath-frosted windowpanes, like Greeks
sketching lines between God-drilled light holes *[handwritten: stars]*

in the night's slate to form one hero *[handwritten: the fathers looking down on them even though they can't always see them]*
of a story, some trace the mutable zodiac

[handwritten: like a gas lamp]

of their fathers' carbide lamps climbing the hill
[handwritten: alcohol] to the tipple. Others wait for the shift whistle
[handwritten: a structure to extract products for transport from a mine]

when their fathers trickle down the hill in a dim stagger,
a pour of steel into the path's worn mold, a spike *[handwritten: dim like the stars]*

dripping into a pry bar widening into a pick-axe head.
Together the fathers are a tool, a story for moon-eyed children.

[handwritten: kids don't know their dads but their dads support them]

[handwritten: too busy drinking to spend time with their kids]

[handwritten: power dynamic—dad is the hero]

I Wake to Find I Am Not Awake

It's still our bedroom—
the books stepping downward
on your nightstand, antacids
and electric fan on mine, you mumbling
French lessons to your class

in your sleep. On the floor,
the sliver of light from the bathroom
streaks your wedding dress even whiter.
My father isn't buttering a brick
with his trowel at the footboard.

Old lovers don't call me into the closet.
The ceiling is neither the infinity
from which I've fallen nor the sum
of my sins crashing upon me.
There is only the queer lurch

and swag of time clouding the surfaces
of my recurring dream
where the thick doors
I've methodically locked behind me
are now ajar.

The Cleaving

The lizard's tail is merely the Devil's gambit.
The moth's unblinking, fragile eyes—goggling

from its flattened wings on the birch and cherry trunks;
the hognose's trick, puffing to strike, a hawser,

a sheepshank poorly tied; crouched leopards rippling
their spots, swishing their tails; the scherzo from farrows

fighting for teats; racemes of celosia,
hosta, and salvia all flaming colors;

even the beetles rolling their dung balls;
dung pile, the chickweed, fescue comprising it,

the iridescent flies lighting, spilling,
the plover pecking grubs, larvae from it,

the organisms, fiddler worms reducing
the mass to soil, the terse refinement,

the compost, fertile dust from which I was conjured—
all matter I thus renamed when cast from Eden.

Abba, you should have pulled me from the void,
drawn the translucent earth and frigid heavens,

and from your reddened knee—where I would have grown
lonely, imagining the platypus

and the sloth's stone face and slow ascent—birthed Eve.

Return to Steinhatchee

No sunset hovered over the bay as I remembered it, no ecstatic
     reds and pinks,
          only no-see-ums

and rain clouds. Your touch had changed too,
          as had mine.

You caressed me the way our daughter, twenty years ago,
          touched her old dog,

which I should have put down a couple of months before, or as
          Dante,
               nearing the third circle,

might have petted the wiry hide of Ciacco the pig, might have
          offered him,
               instead of Cerberus, shovelfuls of black dirt,

or maybe Virgil's honey cake, remembering when Beatrice's
          prophecy
               lay like the cartography of a thigh

sloping gently to calf, her ankle and curled toes the relief of ter-
          rain ahead.
               South, the seagulls swarmed

above trawlers coming in with the tide, the bycatch forming a
          slick of scales and oil
               in the wakes as they passed.

On the dock, a ratty heron with one eye skulked to the fish-
       cleaning table
  where I had left a few sand trout

for the crab traps. With his beady eye upon us, he snatched a
       fish
  like a priest plucking the ear of an altar boy.

Ashes and Dust

"Wherefore I abhor myself, and repent in dust and ashes."
                                                                    —Job 42:6

The reverend presses a thumb
to my forehead, draws a crucifix with ash
from the coal stove
instead of last year's palms—
You must identify with Christ,
his suffering, his withdrawal into the wilderness.

Crossed Jesus stares over his shoulder
at the silk eggs and dusty wings
in the cobweb dangling from the ceiling.
His body conforms to the cross
the way clematis winding a hackberry
climbs for light, submits to its shape,
its obstinacy, and grows into the trunk
becoming the tree. All I can see
is how it must have been: the body's rage
twisting against the cross
like pyracantha loosening the nails
that bind its falling.

I want to take this oiled figure
outside into the sun and rain, into the clouds
of coal dust from the tipple that settle on us all.
I want the body weathered gray
and covered in soot, wood warped
and splintered, nails rusted,
staining buckled wrists and forearms.
Otherwise, I'll abhor no flesh that is mine.

Almost Clean

Knees patched with inner tube,
tomorrow's coveralls stiffen on the line.
Today's boil in a kettle next to the collards.
My father's body, taut as wire, hunches
over a washtub, face black with dust.

His body wears the repentant purple
of Lent after every shift of work.
I wear this smudge of ash, the reverend's
dry kiss marking my withdrawal
from the world. The whistle sounds,

and the graveyard shift begins their clean
descent into the ground. I wash my father's back.
He turns, wipes the ash from my forehead
with his wet palm, looking out the window
at light spreading like water over the slate dump.

In the evening, the moon rises from the river,
curling across dirty sky. Then it drops
behind the bluffs, slips back into the channel,
tumbling all day along the bottom in the current,
around the bend, past Cattail Slough all the way up

to the ferry, until it falls into that deep hole
off Mashburn Point. The crawfish
and minnows pick at what's left
of the night's stain. The next evening
the moon floats up again, bone white.

16

(handwritten annotations:)
stiffen / unwash out the dust
tool
doesn't want this for his child
like a washing machine
clean
death
The moon's path is parallel to the miners' path

Worm Grunters

In Sopchoppy, Florida, they've been waiting all spring
for the wild azaleas to drop their blooms,

for the bluegills to move from their deep haunts
to the creeks and sloughs where they stack up to spawn,

and when fishermen who will pay three bucks
for two dozen night crawlers come calling,

grunters stake ground their grandfathers showed them
late at night. They sit on five-gallon buckets,

drawing leaf springs from old tractors across
black gum stobs like fiddlers groaning over their sins.

You rise to their trembling invocation,
rustling up through the bones of their kin.

Darwin Dreams of the Second Coming

"The Messiah will come only when he is no longer necessary."

—*Franz Kafka*

A shriveled priest shovels
manure and peat into the hole

he spent all day digging
and slips in, burying

himself up to his neck.
His crabapple eyes

roll out of their sockets.
Toes swell to tubers,

ears to budding legumes.
He lures insects

with a sticky tongue, unfolds
its length to catch raindrops

until it falls limp,
detaches, slithers away.

Toilet Flowers

Egyptian women tied papyrus fibers
into Isis knots, damming the moon blood,
the open wound from Thoth, and farther east,
girls watched their mothers wrapping theirs
out of the same thin paper
from which they folded swans,
and later, a man designed the "catamenial [monthly] device,"
and a man called it tampion—a plug for a cannon,
keeping out dust and moisture.
My high school girlfriend called it *George;*
she'd say, "George is in town this week"
when I walked my fingers up her thigh.
But at ten, I knew none of this.
They sat in an open box next to the toilet
I shared with my three brothers, father,
and mother. They didn't come with Mother's warnings
or reprimands like "Don't swordfight with the plunger;
_____ will kill you; _____ will make you go blind."
I knew they were for her; all else was a mystery.
So one Sunday morning while my family
still slept, I latched the bathroom door,
peeled back the wrapper as if it were a popsicle,
and held the plunger: a cannon, a gun barrel.
I pulled on the string, holding the pledget like a mouse
by its tail. I smelled it, pressed my thumbnail
into its soft density, placed it on the sconce like a candle.
Pretending to light it, I threw it into the tub
like an M-80, imagined Gabriel
or Michael lighting the fuse
with the red punk of their pupils

then tossing the pure white scourge at Satan.
I opened another, then three, four,
more and more, holding them in the corner
of my mouth while squinting one eye
like my father chewing his cigar,
tucking them like grenades
into the waistband of my skivvies.
One fell into the toilet and slowly opened
like a moonflower, burgeoning
to life the way I imagined the sea monkeys in ads
on the back cover of my comics would.
I dropped all of them in, one by one,
watching as they bloomed in the bowl.
My mother's footsteps, her voice
behind the door—and I flushed them.
The water rose, spilling over the porcelain lip.
And when I faced my mother—the bathroom
now flooded—I felt shame
for her secret I thought I now knew,
for the beauty I had created
and the sin of creating it.
Adamah, Adam, me, bloody loam.

Magritte's Daemon

René, don't turn your back to me.
Pull your ear from the gramophone,
take off your derby and black mackintosh,
loosen your knickers. You can hang me

in your armoire; I'll always kick the door open.
You can cover my head with a dinner napkin
as if I were cold peas and carrots.
I know your tricks.

My eyes are the eggs you're so fond of,
the ones that neither hatch nor spoil.
When you leave the parlor,
the two pelota players

trace with their cestas
the maple grains emanating from my hip.
They know my age.
When you tightened the laced collar

with your brush, slipping me into that Puritan frock
under the boughs heavy with colorful birds,
did you really believe
I wouldn't take a bite out of one?

Wild Kingdom

My wife talks me into leaving
the guest room pink, just in case
we have a girl. She's itching
to sew a cover for the window seat.
I set up our bed across from the indentations
in the carpet where the couple
before us conceived their children.
I refuse to use the same nail holes
for our mirrors. I move the cable lines
to the opposite corners
of the rooms. In the sunroom,
my wife has hung the stained glass
her father made for her when she was a child;
the lilies and lotus
glow in the morning sun.
She says we need to have sex
at least three times today.
Last night she slept
with a pillow under her butt.

I unpack an old tape
of *Wild Kingdom* episodes.
As a kid, I never understood Jim
after I figured out that Marlin
wasn't his father: every Sunday
squaring off with a walrus
or tangled in the diamonds
of a boa or jumping from a helicopter
onto the back of an elk in snow-capped Montana.
Twisting his white moustache,

Marlin would say, "Jim, go wrestle
that gator," and Jim would lope
to the edge of the swamp.
When I was twelve, I climbed three stories
of scaffolding with a square of shingles
on my shoulder for my father's
one-eyed, Lucky-lipped "That's my boy."

A gray fox—mangy head, tail as bare
as a mimosa switch—rolls across our yard,
stretching its neck and scratching its ears,
until it lifts its nose and bolts.
From backyards, dogs sound
its journey all the way to the river.
A skink suns on the front steps,
its tail an electrical arc.
A wren works a blue ribbon
into our hanging fern:
a few minutes later a twig then a leaf,
a twig then a leaf.
The begonias perfectly circling
the mailbox need watering.
I'll follow the fox instead.

Hamlet beside the Stream

Cruel Fortune, cattail braids, hydrilla tail,
I see you stalk the swan, her lotus neck,
her downcast eyes. The stones below are washed
of fissures, scars, their place of birth. From the womb,
my heir would start to pock and leak.
Beneath the stream's insinuating ripples,
where eddies hold the dead, where leeches wait
and lampreys nibble scales and flesh from host,

the sowbugs scuttle, feeding on hyacinth's
decaying leaves and bloated roots detached
from banks. As April gnaws on winter's sick
and courtiers wring out your amber hair
then close your eyes, I press my palms in clay,
cursing the god who made our hungers weeds.

Coaxing the Coal Back to Life

Some call the concoction a depression plant, but my nanny says
she's coaxing the coal back to life—the same way my grandfather
mixed water and carbide, dropped a gravel stone into his lamp
to make the sunshine he rarely saw. When the leaves fall from
the sparse line of cottonwoods and the only colors are the green
needles of knee-high scrub pines struggling with the overburden,
the older pines dropping daily for pulp and roof chocks, she
gets her wedding vase down from the shelf above the stove,
dusts it off, and mixes the recipe:

6 tablespoons salt
6 tablespoons water
1 heaping spoon ammonia
a couple squirts of mercurochrome
and a few drops of food coloring

She sends me out to fetch a handful of coal from the seam
splintering the bank behind the livery stable, though there's
coal in the bucket next to the stove. Fingering pieces into the
glass vase, a few at a time until she up piles a small cairn, she
pours the purple liquid over the coal. A few days later, the
black mound starts to crystallize and shines like a prism: cran-
berry lace gills, butterscotch carp roe, pewter channel-cat skin,
teal bream beard, mimosa's pink pappus, the skink's indigo
flame.

25

Overburden

A hen squats in the shadow
of my hand, raises tail feathers,
mistaking me for the rooster
I held to the block last night.

Next door, just moved in, a woman picks
at the overburden. A boy, almost old enough
for the mine, speaks Russian to her from the back porch—
his legs severed clean at the knee by the stoop's shadow,

the shadow from her hat brim lifting from a veil
into a blindfold as she raises her head.
A hawk circles the house rows, suspends
in an updraft, swoops down, its shadow a mirage of rich soil.

On Speaking with an Old Schoolmate after His Physics Lecture at a Local University

Despite the intent behind the broom handle,
spokes ticking off the bicycle wheel
like milliseconds from an atomic clock,
the yellow hyphens in the center of the road
linking constants and inertia,
compliance of steel and rubber and asphalt,
friction of skin and bone: how matter vibrates,
compresses, splinters for one common end,
leaving its signature in broken trajectories of light
across a caved-in windshield,
you said you only remembered
a cat's-eye marble rolling slowly toward your cheek,
green swirl corkscrewing from the glass orb
and unraveling across the curb
where you landed. "Kids," you chuckled,
and in those words you forgave us again
just as you always did our transgressions
of loogies and wedgies,
green-pinecone-and-dog-shit bombs.
After the stainless pins, the cast
with your preacher's and parents'
wishes scrawled across it,
the grafts from the small of your back,
the exercises with pinto-bean cans,
you traded us your Mickey Mantles,
encased as if rare specimens defying entropy,
for our abused Niekros and Fisks.

After our "you're all right for a geek,"
after you had turned your back to us,
cradling your atrophied arm at your chest,
we pelted you with the apples
our mothers had packed so lovingly for us.

Elegy for Jessica Hayden

Whacking each other with our recorders,
we descended into the basement for music class.
The pipes above us thumped and hummed.
Toilets flushed. Nina Simone languished in Paris,
her dress yellowing on the sweaty wall.
When Sara Knutson, voice of the class,
asked the teacher why she wore a head scarf,
she told us she was a genie. She pulled out
a white sheet, and we cut it into rectangles,
wrapped them around our venial heads,
as if we could grant wishes to Ms. Hayden
that the doctors could not.
She asked if we had ever tasted our names,
and we began with hers, holding the sibilant of *Jess*
on our tongues like Red Hots, coughing a quick,
repugnant *ic*, and droning the long exhale of *aaah*.

Offerings

"For beauty is nothing but the beginning of terror."
                                        —*Rainer Maria Rilke*

Every so often a tiny hillock appears beside the front porch
where I kicked over the last one: no anthill, no discernable utility,

more like a fresh burial, or an offering of dirt as soft and fine
as the dust collecting in the communion cup

from my wedding. Whatever ruminates
the soil does so with its hollow morel horn sifting the flecks

of my skin, my wife's eyelash and crumbs from her late lunch,
and consuming them, pushing the refuse

into a heap with its wide, crescentic chin. The creature waits
for my footsteps, the front door slamming behind me,

then knock knees up from its ancient cave, circling its chest
with its burgundy claw—as if some kind of genuflection—

before a hurdy-gurdy crank, a gold doubloon,
my feathered crappie jig, my wife's red button

that it has pressed into the soft clay walls. It bows
beneath the hot breath of the dryer vent

and, in a pitch the world has long forgotten, praises
the glistening mound of my car, dewy and warm like a
                newborn god.

Mine Rats

They're always behind you
just beyond the light—
hugging the coal rib and cribbing [child]

timbers, squeezing in [trapped because they can't squeeze in and out of the cracks]
and out of cracks, searching
for what's been lost or discarded:

trolley wire, safety tags,
fuses, canary feathers.
Once, in a dynamite box,

a miner found a nest
made of chewed scripture [scared so bring this for feeling safe]
and company scrip. — [trapping workers because it can only be spent on company goods]

A quick turn or yawn
and you might catch one
in your headlamp's glare

on the shaft collar
or tucked in a kerf
sitting back on its haunches,

eyes burning coal,
spit-shining its face
with licked palms.

One old-timer still pitches
pie crust to shadows. [respects the rats respecting things that are often neglected]
He says the rats [going insane]

31

can feel Mary Lee #1 → who
shudder, hear roof chocks
buckling under her weight,

*the cats known when the
mine is about to collapse*

and when it happens,
he will follow
dragging tails

trusts the rats not the company

and grinding teeth
out of the shadows,
down the chosen path. ← *death*
death is an escape

*so they're bad and gross but
they're a necessary evil.*

*rats are symbolic of something
psychological going on in the miners' heads*

Eden's Oranges

The women didn't ask any questions, just loaded them
from the relief crates in aprons and hurried home.

Because of their size, one woman said they were oranges picked
from orchards in Eden, and the name stuck.

Momma cut one, smooth peel open, pink like candy on the
        inside.
I spit the gristly, sour mush into my hand.

The next day Eden's oranges lined every windowsill in camp.
Some boiled them like potatoes and made marmalade.

Others scooped out the pulp and fried it.
All week we waited for them to ripen.

The day they started to mold, I sat at the table
with a bowl of beans, spreading lard on the last tear of bread.

Momma thanked God for Roosevelt *and* Hoover, for our
        unworthy bodies
and His precious fruits, smiling after every sickly sweet wedge.

After Bloody Mary's Death

"Never think you Fortune can bear the sway
Where virtue's force can cause her to obey."

—*Elizabeth I*

She knelt that day beneath a gangling oak
beside November's swollen River Lea,

away from Hatfield's silver looking glass,
the set of virginals beside her bed,

the dusty Latin books on women's frailty,
away from bordered paths and dying gardens:

acanthus, hyssop, mallow gone to seed
and blackened buds of frost-nipped royal roses.

The water rushed against the rigid bank,
and she, as still as ice, her hair the tinge

of fallen leaves, escaped her courtiers' eyes,
ignored the lords of council. Their pleas for mercy

echoed through orchards, through the hornbeam maze.
Attendants scoured the courtly stables, hay lofts,

her childhood place beyond the suckling foals.
Her withered nursemaid calmly dripped the whites

from eggs, crushed alum, borax, poppy seeds,
mixing her lady's lotion. Humming ballads

and madrigals, her waiting-woman polished
the tarnished orb and crown of Anne Boleyn.

She knelt as if it were a common day.
The land was orphaned. She would pour the milk.

Back Door

After Andrew Wyeth's Wood Stove

The sun lashes an empty rocker.
Geraniums stretch in their puny pots,

nosing the swollen window
where children once waited for the storm

of their father to pass.
A back door remains half sketched.

The kindling bucket
and firewood cradle are bare.

The stove will fall through the floor.
No, the door is disappearing.

Reclamation

The storm defies everything.

Clouds wangle the day into early submission.
The rain never forgets,

cuts worry lines where streams ran
before blasting buried them, carries

silt and seed down to hills
now stripped into valleys.

Valleys piled into hills
settle, consume themselves inch by inch.

Pulp pines creep
to the crumbling edge of a ridge,

already top heavy, drawn like bows
from leaning to the light.

Tulips and Pigs

The tulips were opening up
in front of the hotel,
and we saw each other noticing them.
Sausage kings and pig farmers
here for the pork conference
waited to get brats
from the world's largest grill—
a tanker truck cut in half
and hinged so it would open
like a hotdog bun.
I said, "Want-to-be writers
and pork people all
in the same hotel—
we're all pitching slop."

We walked down to the river
and sat on the riprap, drinking coffee.
An old fisherman in a johnboat
baited his Clorox jugs
and pitched them in the current.
The white jugs disappeared in the glare.
Floating downriver,
he became thin as a crowbar.
We talked about how our children
hated ballet and piano lessons.
We talked about our spouses
more than we should've had to.

Over drinks, I read all of the walls—
the floods and prohibition,

the old jazz clubs on 18th and Vine,
that Boss Tom bought
the Kansas City police,
and that Hot Lips Page
and Charlie Bird scorched
their first brass in this bar
Tom once owned.
When the bartender asked us
if we were married, we looked
at one another and said yes.
We didn't say not to each other.

The Other Woman

I don't, I don't know if I can do it—
the distance between us thin as the lids
hiding your eyes, thin as the cloth

against the belly of your wrists—*again;*
I'm tired of healing—the raised
cuticle on your index finger, the wrinkled brow

of your knuckle—*There's something*
bad wrong with me—I lean into you
the way a broken man leans into his Bible,

pressing his cheek to the filigree, running
the cleft of his chin along the fold
of the raised spine, damp lip blurring

God's promises, blistering vows,
wilting all the crisp unalterables.

Charter

Hundred miles out, after a night of soaking squid for swords—
no swords—everyone's packed in the berth like wasps in a comb
except me on the stern and the mate in the wheelhouse.

The sun swells on the horizon's back. The sea coughs up
bonito; flying fish launch and crash like cheap balsa gliders.
Skiing over wakes, doll-eyed speed trollers skeet fantails,

stippling contrails of bubbles. Below—black contracting
in a sweep of blue—something's balling up ballyhoo.
The mate's "starboard," the throttle pulled back hard,

and the 130's drag plate mewls its aubade, and the marlin
        responds
by tail-walking, shadow-jousting, then sounds, and with
every crank she comes to me too easy—a surge, a pluck of her,

then she's gone, till I reel in what she gave up, hold her hooked
        eye
in my palm: a bocce ball, a boiled swan egg, if anyone could be
        so cruel,
the dark gulf between us as wide as her pupil refusing to shrink
        in the light.

Gauguin's Bed

Between the sky and us, there should be nothing
except the high, frail roof of pandanus leaves

where lizards build their nests. The slender legs
of the moon and bamboo before us disentangle,

then rise at equidistant intervals
beside my bed: reedpipe of the ancients, *vivo*,

unraveling the sounds of night. Silence!
I want the silence before the "signets of hell,"

the dark tattoos, were pricked into the cheeks of women
who now, ghastly in their decrepitude,

prepare the little pigs behind their huts.
I still smell flowered tiaras the women wore

in their pirogues, see their strong bare feet stirring
dust on the paths to their lovers' huts. I craved

that silence in you too, Tahitian princess—absinthe
at your crude lips, your hair a wild myth—sitting

here on my bed, until you said, "La Fontaine,
his morals are ugly—the ants . . . ugh. But the crickets,

yes, yes, to sing, to sing, always to sing!"

Mountain of Fire

The first time the mountain flared,
Widow Caldwell sat on her porch, face covered.

Every couple of weeks the spoil pile would shift
and erupt, a temple of fire, black smut   *not volcanoes*

rising unhindered in braids,
sulfur yellowing our clothes,

coating our tongues when we prayed.   *she lost her husband*
For once, we all wept together.   *in the mines*

Widow Caldwell told anyone who passed
this was Hell's unveiling, the pickaxe the key   *they are their own*
      undoings

to the bottomless pit, the hardened blood of Satan.
"Look to the sky," she said,
      symbolic of Satan world ending

where the whores of Babylon fan the flames."

*mining produces flamable gases
so sometimes they pump it out and
burn it*

*Babylonians enslaved the Jews
The Mining company enslaved its workers*

"La mar es una puta"

Beside the landing, a driftwood cross refuses to age.
The tide is moving in. A sheet of fiddler crabs
wrinkles and sags, unfolds and folds across the sand.
The water boils with herring fry, a city's worth

of wishes, tossed dimes. Seagulls drop, spreading like napkins.
A woman collecting conchs and whelks in a white bucket
maroons herself on a bar. Her husband, a volunteer
for the state, pulls down his mask: "I told you so," he yells,

before he wades to help her in. He's been belt-sanding
"some dirty words in Spanish" from the pavilion eaves.
A half a century ago, sloops, schooners anchored
this horizon. Cuban spongers in dinghies drifted out

of this shallow cove with the tide, the orange sun melting
into white breakers before them, sky inflamed, inflamed.

Floundering

1.

When the tides were right
outside of Pass Christian, I would see them
heron-stalking the shallows, gigs held high

in one hand, a lantern in the other.
They were tracking beds, depressions where flounders
had ambushed a mullet or mud minnow

and had settled back down a couple yards away,
leaving nothing behind but cloudy water
and the imprints of their bodies.

2.

They bury their bodies into the dirty bottom,
waiting for prey, accepting
the coarse sand and silt

like monks accepted hair shirts,
waited for some sign of luminous grace
to hover above them

and take their hungers away.
They expose only the black pearls
of their catywampus eyes,

one nested between the gill plate
and jagged teeth, the other lurking
at the edge of their mottled, spade-shaped head

since the eye seeped through the body
to merge with the other
when they were just fry,

condemning them to vision always fixed
upward and to the terrible weight of the world.
Perhaps they don't scurry

when the giggers find them because they've conceded
the shallow graves of their bodies while in awe
of the light spreading above them,

and, perhaps, in those barbed seconds,
they're bucking in the ecstasy
of their flesh rising into the impaled air.

On Reading Huckleberry Finn

I handed him the ratchet extension and three-eighths socket,
then, after he bloodied his knuckles trying to break loose a met-
ric nut on the catalytic converter, the cheater bar and vice grips.
My friends pedaled by, leaving a contrail of dust behind their
Western Flyers: fishing rods held like jousting poles and nothing
but red-eyed bass ahead.

That night, under a sheet, holding my flashlight, I slopped in
the untamed Mississippi. The yellowed paper smelled like the
basement, like the river and pipe smoke coursing through its
pages. Like Tom, I didn't care much about church. God was
Huck's Pap, a dead-beat dad, and the preacher's sedated Jesus,
all love and forgiveness even when they nailed him up.

Later that week, Daddy woke me up, holding a trotline and a
tub of livers. We pushed the Datsun down the driveway and
popped the clutch. Wading the Cahaba as a storm moved in, we
ran a stringer of Appaloosas before dawn. Our bodies covered
with grey mud, arms burning from stinging nettle, Daddy gut-
ted the catfish on the front porch, and I flipped the kicker, a
soft-shelled turtle, on its back, trying to tempt its head out from
under the carapace. That morning Mama ironed every wrinkle
from her favorite dress and strapped on her white sandals so
she could go hear about Judgment Day. She never said a word
to us.

Stake Horse

After the finals
of the world nine-ball tournament,
Cannonball clipped the nipple in the back room,
a perfect miss, the ball
teetering on the rim of the corner pocket.

Daddy dumped the nine,
then talked Cannonball's friend—
who'd "never played them
fancy games," but upped
the ante anyway—into one pocket.

I was ten, running single malts
and champagne for Mr. Mapo,
our oil tycoon, with his twenty-dollar
gold piece as a belt buckle
and his lady friends as sequined
and toothy as barracudas.

His bulldog licked his fat thumb,
telling me to keep the change,
which I funneled to Daddy,
who by then had spat
on his wedding band,

trying to twist it off his finger.
Through the smoke, ladies dangling
from his hips, Mapo looked like a Hindu god.
His bulldog handed me
Mapo's number and a cue in a leather case.

Ahead of us, we had a pack of bologna
in the station wagon, forty miles
of I-10 to the local pool hall, and the neon stars
of pawn shops and liquor stores ushering us home
to the Ho Jo where I hoped Mama still slept.

The Mule

When he was young,
he'd just as soon stomp a stalking coyote
as back-kick a newborn calf.
Before this sterile prince of the pasture
was gagged, strapped,
and led down the shaft
where time is measured by wear on the bit,
he pissed on fescue
and browsed through barbed wire on privet.

Down here he's just another jack
taking the same steps
in the same ruts,
then back again for another load.
Behind a blindfold,
pupils spreading like ink to the edge,
there's no world left in his eyes.

He hopes this longer haul upward
is only a dream.
The hoarse *Gee, Haw,* and *Hooooo,*
straps kneading against hames,
the creaky wheel—are deadened to whispers
by sledges pounding fresh track up ahead.
Nearing the surface, he shivers
and swats his tail at the warmth
as he once swatted flies.
A tinge of honeysuckle
smells sour as skunk.
He recoils at the light

flashing around his blinders,
stumbles toward a ring of fire
he can't bear.

Grabbing

For weeks, we've been slopping the catfish
with offal the butcher can't sell, wading out
waist deep into the slough to sink hollow logs
with rocks. Daddy kneels down
in the mud, bowing into the river.
A gray cloud stirs the surface.

He juts up through the slick, arm nearly elbow deep
in a flathead, and fingers out the gills.
Nailing it to a cedar between the eyes,
he rips the white belly, scoops out a handful
of entrails, pliers exposing the white flesh,
while the body bucks trying to swim up the tree.

Sundays, Mama amens the preacher's stained armpits
and his thin index finger,
the trials and burdens, Jesus's strong back
and our eternal guilt, and thanks God for all
we don't have and don't deserve.
She clanks what's left from a week's mining
back into the polished plate of the company church.

Methane

I. Whistle

[handwritten: ← bird sexually immature male wild turkey]

A tricked jake
scratching under a white oak fans out,
shudders, pushes out his chest
and gobbles back. A teacher

and most of her students
stop mid-sentence; four or five
continue the cadence: 5 − 3 = 2, 4 − 3 = 1 . . .
A young woman drops a bottle

[handwritten: in school summer disruption — some of the kids' fathers don't work in the mines]

of bleach at the company commissary.
The night shift rolls over,
squints in afternoon sunlight.
They know the whistle

[handwritten: stanzas don't end in periods — no one knows what's going on]

should wake them only
in the darkness to work the mine;
in the daylight, it screeches cave-in
or methane. A Greek woman pries

[handwritten: Greek fire]

the lids from Mason jars,
raises a butter crock in the well,
while the town scrambles
down to the slope mouth.

[handwritten: almost a normal occurance]

She rolls dough for pierogies,
crimps kraut and prunes inside,
drops the square pies in boiling water,
waits for them to bloat and rise to the surface.

[handwritten: ← Ukranian/Polish]

[handwritten: preparing funeral foods]

[handwritten: like methane bubbles — dead miners rising to the surface]

53

2. Extraction

Mahoney goes in first,
checks the flame in his safety lamp.
"Itty bitty blue you're through," he says,
waves us in.

The first body kneels
against the coal rib, his back to the blast,
face nuzzled in the wing of his elbow
when the after damp took him.

The upper half of another,
rock, and scrap
must have shot a quarter mile
down the shaft like lead
from a shotgun barrel.
His eyes still goggle
from the flight.

We throw torsos over our shoulders,
gather the rest in buckets and sacks.

Doc spreads them out in a line,
looks for safety tags on those with clothes.
He measures feet and starts matching pairs,
presses palms together in the lamplight,
checks lengths of fingers, remnants of nails
and grit underneath.
Kuzma counts one extra.

stanzas and in periods, things are final

images of wealth

praying

dirt or courage?

matching dead with who they were

54

Some Like It Hot

Marilyn must have washed off the lollipop
in her last shot glass of whisky. Swishing from the hotel
to the dock,

she's pushing her bias-cut dress to its limits. Her love interest
promises a yacht full of pillows and wave crests
white as toothpaste.

On the television screen, the moon
is just as high and temporary
as it is outside my window.

Moonlight hits her soft shoulders the same way
it hits the slate roof of the birdfeeder and the standing water
where I overwatered the begonias.

My wife is upstairs, unpacking
her winter clothes, though she knows
the seasons

never really change in Florida. She'll start making chili in
        November.
Like last year, after the move, she'll tell me she admires the
        names
Ezra and *Susanna.*

Marilyn, can't you see he's just another horn player?
I'll fall asleep on the couch before the end, as I always do,
not knowing if a bucket of sea shells, instead of Shell Oil, will
        please her.

Mayflies

Ripples pinprick the surface.
It's coming from below,
mayfly nymphs pipping,
twitching out of skins,
and fanning moist wings. A few
then tens of thousands
rise in frenzied clouds.
Males fall first,
drizzling back to the water's face
like ash, then females light
the shining and spill their eggs
before night takes over.

Here I am at the quarry
again, thinking of stories to tell you:
the raccoon that made off
with the hotdog buns, the broken
tent pole, the cottonwoods someone
cut and hauled off to sell
for violin bridges in Japan or China,
the bald eagle nesting in a loblolly,
the gobbler strutting in a green field,
all of the things I didn't see
yesterday or today, but instead
remember from when I was a kid,
the observations you say bring us closer.
I won't tell you about the mayfly nymphs,
the urge for change, flight, and sex; how,
nonetheless, the nymphs wait patiently for years

in the dark cracks of riprap and sunken leaves
for the perfect day, temperature, clarity;
how nights with her make me love you more.

Take Over

Mourning doves fatten on power lines.
The rocker hums, bees boring into the armrests.

Virginia creeper sags in the breeze
below the eaves. The scraggly heads

of pine seedlings peer from gutters.
Ivy covers the burn barrel, my old bicycle,

chicken coops, satellite dish, igniting across a cord of wood,
then rears, flaring up through the kennel's chain-link fence.

Ants spiral up the climbing tree
into the black hole of the bluebird box.

Brick Hammer and Broken Watch

"I'm about as lonesome as a pool ball gets
and there's nothing I can do."
                    —*mishearing of Steve Earle lyrics*

On the back porch, the cat kills another lizard,
bats it around, and kills it again—
until nudging it with his cheeks and temples, wishing
it were alive again, he paws at the sliding-glass door

to come in. My wife braises a chicken—
some recipe she saw on The Food Channel—
complaining of counter space and the small fridge.
After dinner, I'll go upstairs and finish boxing up books

to make room for a nursery. Some are easy:
contemporary ones of which I read only a chapter
or a few poems then put down,
and the best-love-poems anthologies

and multiple copies of Shakespeare's and Browning's
sonnets given to me by relatives for Christmas—
the same relatives who don't understand why
I can't write a jingle for their hardware store

or blessings for their daughters' weddings.
"Well, you can always go back
to cutting grass," they say. I'll box the providence
and prudence of the eighteenth century: Pamela, Moll,

and Evelina begging for love
from a thrift-store shelf. I'll pack the Whitman deathbeds,

I like the 1855 better anyway, and the stack of Bibles
in my closet, again my relatives, except for the one

I keep with my reference books, the one I found
in my mailbox a couple of days after my father died,
marked with Romans verses and "He's calling you to be his son.
He wants you to know him and walk with him."

I visited my father once in fifteen years. I stayed all day
while the wind stirred leaves from the dormant grass.
The leaves were all the same perfect shape
and wet-rust color from the oak my grandfather planted

when his parents died. I couldn't remember his voice,
only his words—"Keep your pecker in your pants, boy.
You don't want any younguns now;
I know." I could see him laughing,

followed by the eye-watering coughing fit,
when he watched *All in the Family*,
and on Saturday mornings on the couch,
with a paper in his lap, cleaning car parts,

pool-cue chalk still on his nose
from the night before. I kept only
his brick hammer, which I use to pry and bang on things
I can't fix, as he did, and a broken Gucci watch

he took off a drunk in a game of one-pocket.
I brought a handful of rice for the anthills
anchored to my family's headstones:
some old country remedy about the workers

leaving after the rice stops up
the queen and she bloats and dies.
I couldn't find any when I stomped the mounds.
I thought there was nothing left to kill.

wishing he could kill something

she remorseful or annoyed that he can't kill them anymore

The father is dead but was he really alive before?

burying memories

The Motel Room

My mother had taken off the shirt-waist dress
she had to wear to classes and slipped on bellbottoms
to walk from the Baptist college to town.
It could've been the ride he offered her to the drugstore

in his shark-finned '58 Impala. It could've been the date
he claimed to have later that night with a woman
whose black hair fell to her waist, or it could've been
the stiff cowboy hat she'd seen only on television.

It was the Fourth of July, and most of the students
had gone home. It could've been because he didn't know
about Ovid's "Echo and Narcissus,"
or because he didn't go on his date with the racy woman;

it could've been because he waited instead on his porch
until after dark she passed again with a sailor.
It couldn't be because two days later he took her
with a six-pack to a motel room for their first date,

or because her stepmother sent her down from Chicago
to Birmingham for her step-grandparents' wedding anniversary,
or because, while there, she had secretly enrolled in college,
or because she had no one left but my father to please.

an affair?

Mantrip

Before dawn, waiting
for the mantrip creaking up
the railed tongue of Mary Lee
to return them underground,
old-timers, Hungarian Slavs,
brothers, blasters, nap on a bench,

stubby arms folded across their chests,
legs out straight, propped
on dinner buckets—tiered urns
filled with weak coffee and goulash—
in their laps dynamite boxes and
tamping sticks whittled out of birch,

snap-brims pulled down
over their eyes, heads cocked to the east
away from the yawning mouth of the mine,
as if Mary Lee had whispered a sacred
lie into the ear of the first,
putting him at ease,

who whispered it in turn
to the next and the next and the next
until the last coughed up the secret,
rising like a cloud of dust
into the chilled night:
The day is in flower.

The Old Salt's Brag

for Frank

*"Unequaled as a partner in battle, her reliability borders
on relentless. To say she is tough is to speak an under-
statement of immeasurable proportions. There is nothing
casual in her lines or timid in her performance."*
                              —Contender Boats advertisement

All I need is a rusty hook dangling from my ear.
I'll swim in the buck out to the Dry Tortugas,
braiding a leader out of chest hair.

I'll whittle my pinky finger to the bone
with a seagull beak and hone it with my heel.
I'll slit my belly with it and unravel a length of gut.

I don't need your lily-white war mistress
with waxed galley and perfumed head,
your Boss Magnum TwinDrag reels

with Joint Strike Fighter aluminum
and aerospace-grade stainless-steel bearings,
your Power Butt rods, touch-screen GPS,

and your polypropylene skivvies.
I'd rather pluck out my good eye,
snap a thumb clean, and butterfly the flesh for bait.

I'll make a rattling teaser out of fingernails.
When I lure that blackfin up,
I'll pull her in hand over hand

and hold her lines up to your world.
I'll tuck her in the corner of my maw
and sink to the bottom where we belong.

Worms: Georg Cantor, From Halle Sanatorium, 1884

Before I pinched you into three equal parts,
you tried to burrow into the creases of my cupped palm.

For years after, I saw you in my mother's auburn curls
when she leaned over me for the Apostles' Creed,

in the mahogany scroll, in the F-holes
of my violin, in the lemniscate my father's finger tips

traced against his temples when I ran the bow
too long or too short. Your twelve hearts vibrated

from the page to the strings, the bridge,
across my cheek, my dry lips during a *col legno*,

and later, when my parents thought I slept,
you were the shivering flame, dripping wax

from the candle that defined their moaning,
and now you return, old ghost, each segment

of you a succulent number in my continuum:
the umbilical cord stretching through

and beyond the omphalos of God. End
without end. End without end. End without end.

Epilogue and Return

"The whole universe is full."

—*Tomas Tranströmer*

A waning moon spreads its last light
across the Warrior River

where slash pines have given way
to beetles and rot.

The homestead chimney
has crumbled into itself: a cairn

for skinks and deer mice.
On high ground next to the trash heap,

a slider backs her rear into a hole
she dug. Every ten minutes

or so a ping-pong ball
breeches and drops. At dusk,

she kicks back dirt with her hind legs
and waddles down to the muddy slough,

never looking back
until next spring when she will claw

at this hill again.
Barges heaped with coal

lumber through another oxbow.
Trains wail their way home.

[handwritten margin notes:] the after affects of humans on the land

the ant queen bloated by the rice

67